THE POCKET BOOK OF
ENGLAND RUGBY

Independent and Unofficial

Edited by

RICHARD BATH

SEVENOAKS

First published by SevenOaks in 2019
An imprint of the Carlton Publishing Group
20 Mortimer Street
London W1T 3JW

A CIP catalogue record for this book is available from the
British Library.

ISBN 978-1-78177-909-5

Printed in Dubai

"I do hope not."

Captain **CARL AARVOLD**, replies to a fan who said, "may the better team win", before England met South Africa in 1932

CHAPTER 1

SWING LOW, SWEET CHARIOT

INTRODUCTION

Rugby is a sport whose defining characteristics include raw passion, brutal honesty and comradeship, all of which are underpinned by an often savage wit. It's a combination which has produced some of the best bon-mots in the sporting world, and none more so than when it comes to the cradle of the game: England.

Whether it comes from the fans, referees, coaches or players, rugby humour is often as high-octane and hard-hitting as the biggest tackle in the heat of a Twickenham international. Whether it's an entertaining case of foot in mouth disease or a withering put-down of a teammate or opponent, there is something for everyone in these pages.

One of my favourites in *The Pocket Book of England Rugby* was Damian Hopley's immortal quip after he heard he was being touted as England's answer to Jonah Lomu ("Me? As England's answer to Jonah Lomu? Joanna Lumley, more likely.") but there are quotes which changed the game too.

When Will Carling talked about the RFU's "57 old farts", for instance, it was an off-camera aside but it came to symbolize much that was wrong with the game and was a catalyst for profound change in the way the game is run.

For those who love Rugby Union, *The Pocket Book of England Rugby*'s verbal treasures will transport you straight back to the games and controversies of the past in a way that no dry history of the game is able to do.

So we hope that you enjoy reading the wit and occasional shards of wisdom in the following pages as much as I enjoyed putting it together.

CONTENTS

"Handling the ball is only a minor part of your job, so don't give much thought to it."

Former England fly-half **DAI GENT**, on forward play in his 1933 book Rugby Football

"In the mid Eighties, selection for England was the modern equivalent of being named as accredited food taster for Attila the Hun."

England fly-half **ROB ANDREW**

"There is far too much talk about good ball and bad ball. In my opinion, good ball is when you have possession and bad ball is when the opposition have it."

Legendary England three-quarter **DICKIE JEEPS**

"This looks a good team on paper, let's see how it looks on grass."

England scrum-half **NIGEL MELVILLE** on England's new look against Australia in 1984

"Everybody thinks we should have moustaches and hairy arses, but in fact you could put us all on the cover of Vogue."

HELEN KIRK on women's rugby teams, 1987

"I knew he would never play for Wales ... he's tone deaf."

VERNON DAVIES, a Welshman, in 1981 on his son
Huw's choice to play for England and not Wales

"I don't know why prop forwards play rugby."

LIONEL WESTON in 1974

"The tactical difference between Association Football and Rugby, with its varieties, seems to be that in the former, the ball is the missile; in the latter, men are the missiles."

ALFRED E. CRAWLEY, The Times' rugby correspondent in 1913

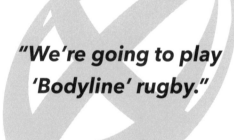

"We're going to play 'Bodyline' rugby."

EDDIE JONES, England coach, ramps up the aggression before England head down to his native Australia on tour

"Of all the teams in the world you don't want to lose to, England's top of the list. If you beat them it's because you cheat. If they beat you it's because they have overcome your cheating."

GRANT FOX, All Black fly-half

"The backs preen themselves and the forwards drink."

A truism of the game from **DEAN RICHARDS**

"Playing in the second row doesn't require a lot of intelligence really."

BILL BEAUMONT, if anyone would know, it would be the former England captain and second row

"Once you're on the pitch it's chaos. I find it faintly amusing this view that some people have of the captain, clicking his fingers and saying 'Guys, let's try Plan B', and everyone goes 'Oh God, yes, Plan B'. That's bollocks."

England captain **WILL CARLING**

"All we're doing effectively is chasing a pig's bladder around a field but we have the ability to touch so many people."

JOSH LEWSEY, England World Cup-winning full-back

"A lot of people think prop forwards are just dumb animals but front-row play is almost like a game of chess. Besides the physical factor there is a lot of psychological work going on."

JEFF PROBYN, England's undersized but highly effective tight-head prop

"I could never understand why people got so nervous for me. Kicking was my job and it just so happened that I was good at it."

Prolific points scorer **DUSTY HARE**

"I turned my head to look down the tunnel and for the ball and Burton turned his head and opened his mouth as if to bite me."

Hooker **PETER WHEELER** on his England and Lions teammate, prop Mike Burton, when crossing swords for their respective clubs, Leicester and Gloucester

"Goal-kicking is a mixture of technique and temperament. You must try to box up the goal-kicking in a little compartment away from everything else and become a little machine from the moment the whistle goes and a penalty is awarded."

ROB ANDREW, 1989

"It will not be a Korean war, nor a Boer war, nor any other war. It will be 15 men against 15, it will be professionals against professionals."

South African team manager **GIDEON SAM** unsuccessfully attempts to ratchet down fears of another ill-tempered encounter between the Springboks and England

"People think rugby players would make the worst dancers but you would be surprised. Some moves we use to warm up are similar to dancing."

MATT DAWSON, before taking part in *Strictly Come Dancing*

"Wade Dooley: With a handle like that he sounds more like a western sheriff than the Lancashire bobby that he is."

Former Scotland hooker **NORMAN MAIR** on the England and Lions hard man

CHAPTER 2

HEROES OF THE SHIRT

"There he was, half his teeth missing, cheekbones smashed, hair all over the place, his skin looking as if it hadn't seen the sun for six months. He looked like he'd just come out of a bunker. But what a player."

France's **LAURENT CABANNES** on Dean Richards

"I think Brian Moore's gnashers are the kind you get from a DIY shop and hammer in yourself. He is the only player we have who looks like a French forward."

England prop **PAUL RENDALL**

"Me? England's answer to Jonah Lomu? Joanna Lumley, more likely."

England centre **DAMIAN HOPLEY**

"If I had been a winger, I might have been daydreaming and thinking about how to keep my kit clean for next week."

BILL BEAUMONT

"I played ten injury-free years between the ages of 12 and 22. Then, suddenly, it seemed like I was allergic to the twentieth century."

NIGEL MELVILLE in 1984 after a succession of career-threatening injuries

"Being dropped and Take That splitting up on the same day is enough to finish anyone off."

MARTIN BAYFIELD

*"I can't rest until I have tamed
the devil in my head."*

JONNY WILKINSON

"I'm pleased to say that I don't think about rugby all the time, just most of the time."

LAWRENCE DALLAGLIO

"If they're going to call you this superhuman player or whatever and you believe it, then you should also believe it when they call you a tosser."

MARTIN JOHNSON

"Throughout the week I have one side of me that does all the preparation and resting and eating well and training, then it hands over to the second individual and that other individual is a hugely competitive, instinctive one who is just desperate to win. He is a bit of a monster actually."

JONNY WILKINSON

"Dean Richards is named Warren, as in Warren ugly bastard."

JASON LEONARD

"I'm sure the lads will be pleased to see him gone. There will be more food for everyone now."

AUSTIN HEALEY on Jason Leonard's retirement

"He's mad as a cut snake. He plays with a lot of energy, he's emotional, he scores tries, he's a real winner to me."

EDDIE JONES talks up England wing Chris Ashton

"He's got that educated left foot kick - you can tell he's been to public school."

JONES on Wasps back Elliot Daly

"It's the best bullock I've ever had."

Farmer and England hooker **GRAHAM DAWE** on Mr Chilcott, a prize-winning beast on his farm

"I'm short, I don't drink and I don't know the words to any dirty songs. I'm pretty useless really."

WILL CARLING

"I looked up and there was this enormous young lad in Preston Grasshoppers colours. He was so big he blocked the light out."

Ex-England skipper **DICK GREENWOOD** on hard man Wade Dooley

"Deep down, I am still the same miserable old man."

MARTIN JOHNSON on approaching retirement

"We'll probably drink as hard as we train, and that is very hard."

Noted bon viveur **STUART BARNES** looks forward to the 1989 Five Nations

*"I'm just very lazy.
I hate training."*

DEAN RICHARDS

"I was told by Dave Alred [England's kicking coach], 'Do yourself a favour with the hair'. I thought, 'This is ridiculous', but I ended up doing it. It was also suggested to me that if I'd had a better haircut, I'd have probably stayed on the pitch that day."

ANDY GOMMERSALL after being taken off against New Zealand at Twickenham in 2004

"I saw the witch doctor and she said she found out there were three lady spirits who had married themselves on to me for the last three years. The witch doctor told me that was why I had been injured ... They wanted to punish me and injuring me was the way to do it. Every time I played – bang!"

England centre **MANU TUILAGI** explains why he consulted a witch doctor in his family's native Samoa to solve persistent injuries

CHAPTER 3

SVENGALIS & GURUS

"*Arrogance is only bad when you lose. If you are winning and you are arrogant it is self-belief.*"

England coach **EDDIE JONES**

"If I am in a minority of one, it doesn't mean to say that I am wrong."

CLIVE WOODWARD

"I'm not a homosexual but I realise now that I loved Clive Woodward."

France coach **BERNARD LAPORTE**

"Sir Clive (Woodward) summed it up best when he said everyone hates England. And it's true. Because of the history that is involved, the surrounding countries with the social and historical context, that long-seated rivalry – you can feel that hatred of England."

England coach **EDDIE JONES**

"You have 15 players in a team. Seven hate your guts and the other eight are making their mind up."

England coach **JACK ROWELL**

"I'd rather crawl across broken glass naked than speak to Will Carling."

DICK BEST, Carling's former coach at Harlequins and England

"This is going to sit with us all forever – players, coaches, management. I don't think I'll ever come to terms with it personally because it was such a big thing. We lost two games, but they were crucial games and ultimately that let us down."

A depressed England head coach **STUART LANCASTER** on the hosts' early 2015 Rugby World Cup exit

"If you are not physical in rugby, you may as well be playing volleyball or curling."

England coach **EDDIE JONES**

"I handle things the Brian Clough way. Whenever a player has a problem we talk about it for 20 minutes and I listen carefully to what he has to say. Then we'll agree that I was right."

SIR CLIVE WOODWARD

"Let others tell you how good you are; I'll tell you how to get better."

CHALKIE WHITE, Leicester and England coach

"We don't want to have a kava party, we want to eat fish and chips."

EDDIE JONES vows his side will play good old-fashioned "English rugby" against Fiji

"I wasn't satisfied with the World Cup victory. I don't think we played very well in the tournament. We've been very narrow in our approach for the past two years."

ANDY ROBINSON before the first match of his short-lived tenure as England coach, November 2004

"I cannot compromise. Winning is about inches. Look at Kelly Holmes – she won by inches. We won the World Cup by inches. You don't win World Cups by compromising."

CLIVE WOODWARD explains his resignation as England coach

"Clive had lots of ideas. The terrible ones were dropped, the good ones adapted and the great ones we used."

MARTIN JOHNSON on Clive Woodward

"The only place for a coach in rugby is in transporting the teams to the match."

England captain **ERIC EVANS** in 1957

"Dick's way is certainly not my way. Ambitious people aren't really on my wavelength."

MICKEY SKINNER on his relationship with his Harlequins and England coach Dick Best

"Enjoyment and rugby do not go together."

England coach **DICK BEST**

"I'm a great believer in coaching but I believe in players even more. Look back at the great coaches and you'll find they had some great players to work with."

England prop **FRAN COTTON**

"They have the impression of English rugby that we all play in Wellington boots and we play in grass that is two foot long."

SIR CLIVE WOODWARD on the French

"The honour of representing your country has got to be the single most important driving force. The England players will be reminded too that the graveyard is full of indispensable men."

GEOFF COOKE, England coach, 1990

"I have many emotions about my time with England, but that's a story for another time. It's a closed chapter and I'm now looking forward to a new and very broad challenge here."

Sacked England coach **BRIAN ASHTON** starts his new job at the University of Bath

"And there's Beaumont in that English scrum, looking like a man who enjoys his food ..."

BILL McLAREN on Bill Beaumont, the English captain

CHAPTER 4

SIX NATIONS EPICS

"Turn them over. Smash 'em. Simple as that. Relish it. Shut their crowd up, shut their players up. Win the match."

Captain **MARTIN JOHNSON** before the Grand Slam decider against Ireland in Dublin in 2002

"I think my life probably flashed before my eyes. I thought if we lost the game I would have to run straight out of the stadium and get a cab home."

JAMES HASKELL, on being yellow-carded against Ireland in 2003

"The only memories I have of England and the English are unpleasant ones. They are so chauvinistic and arrogant."

France No.8 **IMANOL HARINORDOQUY** does his bit for the *Entente Cordiale*

"Activity and skill were at a discount and very rough play was indulged in by both sides, the brandy bottle having frequently to be requisitioned for the knocked-out ones."

REPORT of England's 5-0 win over Scotland in 1892

"Colin may not have looked too good but I'm told he smelled lovely."

England scrum-half **STEVE SMITH** after prop Colin Smart drank a bottle of aftershave at the England v France post-match banquet in 1982

"It was a rugby player's dream. It was coming to the end of the match and my only contribution had been a dropped pass."

ANDY HANCOCK, England wing, on his last-minute try which gave England a 3-3 draw with Scotland at Twickenham in 1965

"Will Carling nodded at me to ask if I wanted to take them and I indicated that I did. But Brian [Moore] got the ball and said the forwards would run them."

Full-back **SIMON HODGKINSON** on the decision to run two kickable penalties when England lost 13-7 to Scotland in the 1990 Grand Slam decider

"Records have never been a motivation. I'm just prospering from the work of others. I thought about a personal milestone only once last season, after the Welsh game where I scored for the third match running. I thought I might get a try in every Five Nations match. We all know what happened next: Scotland – no grand slam, no try."

RORY UNDERWOOD, in 1991

"They were lucky to get nought."

England coach **GEOFF COOKE** on France after England won 11-0

"Appointing Will as captain two years ago was the best decision we have made. He is the most successful England leader for at least 50 years."

GEOFF COOKE on Will Carling in 1991

"Of all rugger, an ordinary well-contested Calcutta Cup match is beyond all question the cream."

Early 20th century rugby journalist **EHD SEWELL**

"Like hell, England, like hell."

England pack leader **H C "DREADNOUGHT" HARRISON**, on how England should play during the 1914 Calcutta Cup at Inverleith, which they went on to win 16–15

"It was like M*A*S*H in the medical room."

LEON WALDEN, RFU doctor, after the feisty England v Wales game in 1980

"People talk about a jinx but I discount that. England failed to win in Cardiff for a very long time for one simple reason: the Welsh were too good. If we'd had players like Gareth Edwards, JPR Williams, Barry John, Gerald Davies ... then England would have beaten everyone too."

BILL BEAUMONT, in 1991, on England's failure to win in Cardiff since 1963

"Once and for all, I'm not a second Jonny Wilkinson."

CHARLIE HODGSON before England played France at Twickenham in 2005 and he missed a late drop-goal in an 18–17 defeat

"They can talk the talk, but they didn't walk the walk, did they?"

Hooker **RICHARD COCKERILL** after England's 1999 win over Ireland

"An 18-year-old wonder until Saturday and a 19-year-old reject today."

NIGEL MELVILLE, on Matthew Tait, after the teenager endured a torrid debut against Wales in 2005

"I really enjoyed it. I was trying to be as annoying as possible in the scrummage. There were four or five scrums where there were punches coming through. They were obviously going to target me and try to get a reaction, but it's all part of the game."

JULIAN WHITE, England prop, after beating France at Twickenham in 2001

"I felt like dying in the last five minutes. It was knackering. The second half was unbelievable. After about 20 minutes we were calling for the cavalry. It showed how fast the game was because the ref got injured."

AUSTIN HEALEY after England beat France in 2001

"Every time I went to tackle him, Horrocks went one way, Taylor went the other, and all I got was the bloody hyphen."

Ireland's **MICK ENGLAND** on trying to stop Phil Horrocks-Taylor

"We'll take our medicine. It's a massive learning curve. It's a massive character assessment. We've all been there. In 2015 the media were ready to burn us alive and six months later we'd turned it around. Rugby and professional sport, it's the flip of a coin."

JAMES HASKELL has a cliché overload channelling his inner Alan Partridge, as he cites England's 2016 Grand Slam months after their 2015 Rugby World Cup early exit

"We can easily find another 15 players to play Scotland in a month if it proves necessary. What they did was discourteous."

RFU secretary **Dudley Wood** after England players refused to attend a press conference in 1991

CHAPTER 5

RUGBY WORLD CUP HEROICS

"We're going to tear those boys apart."

WILL CARLING's message pinned on the changing room wall before the 1995 World Cup semi-final in Cape Town… New Zealand thrashed England 45-29

"I don't know about us not having a Plan B when things went wrong, we looked like we didn't have a Plan A."

GEOFF COOKE, following England 1995 Rugby World Cup semi-final demolition by New Zealand

"We tried to handle the ball in the wrong places and I blame the media for that."

England coach **JACK ROWELL** on the 1995 World Cup

"Most Misleading Campaign of 1991: England's rugby World Cup squad, who promoted a scheme called 'Run with the Ball'. Not, unfortunately, among themselves."

TIME OUT magazine

"Burgess lacks the sense of timing, in attack and defence, required to be effective at international level. His naivety embarrassed those around him and severely damaged England's chances of reaching the quarter-finals. Stuart Lancaster picked a league convert who doesn't know how to play inside centre."

Ireland's **GORDON D'ARCY** on England's decision to play Sam Burgess against Wales in the 2015 World Cup

"It's just nice that Danny is tweeting about someone other than himself. He's a good bloke and I enjoy his selfies a lot. He can say what he likes, he wouldn't ever be a part of our team."

Wallaby **ADAM ASHLEY-COOPER** responds to Danny Cipriani's comments that no Australia player would make the 2015 England team

"England's coach Jack Rowell, an immensely successful businessman, has the acerbic wit of Dorothy Parker and, according to most New Zealanders, a similar knowledge of rugby."

MARK REASON in 1996

"Remember that rugby is a team game; all 14 of you make sure you pass the ball to Jonah."

ANONYMOUS fax to the All Black team before the 1995 World Cup semi-final against England

"To be truthfully honest with you, I didn't know that bonus points counted in the World Cup. I was just more excited that I'd scored a try."

BILLY VUNIPOLA's late try against Fiji may have earned England a vital bonus point at the 2015 World Cup

"We play a similar style of rugby to England but we have better-looking players."

Springbok hooker **SCHALK BRITS** appeals to England fans to switch their allegiance in 2015 after their pool stage exit

"I could hardly kiss him, could I? We did realise we were hugging each other for a little bit too long though, and moved on to find someone else to do it to."

WILL GREENWOOD after England's 2003 Word Cup win

"It was like the Falklands crisis. I was counting them in and then counting them out."

England coach **JACK ROWELL** on his multiple substitutions against the hard-tackling Samoans in 1995

"Giant gargoyles, raw-boned, cauliflower-eared monoliths that intimidated and unsettled. When they ran onto the field it was like watching a tribe of white orcs on steroids. Forget their hardness, has there ever been an uglier forward pack?"

MICHAEL LAWS, New Zealand politician, on England's 2003 World Cup-winning pack

"It was embarrassing. It won't go on the mantelpiece at home."

JOE LAUNCHBURY, on his Man of the Match award after England lost to Australia in the 2015 Rugby World Cup

"Whether we realised it at the time or not, we had bloody good players, bloody good coaches and a brilliant opportunity to go and do it."

MARTIN JOHNSON, England's World Cup-winning captain a decade after the team's greatest moment

"Will Carling epitomizes England's lack of skills. He has speed and bulk but plays like a castrated bull."

DAVID CAMPESE's damning verdict on England's captain in 1995

"I was going nuts. We kept putting ourselves in trouble, making error after error. But who cares, I thought – we have won the World Cup."

SIR CLIVE WOODWARD

"It's not just the group of death, it's the group of hell."

WARREN GATLAND, Wales coach, after Australia's win over England guaranteed Wales a quarter-finals place

"As you run around Battersea Park in them, looking like a cross between a member of the SAS and Blake's Seven, there is always the lingering fear of arrest."

BRIAN MOORE on the 1995 England Rugby World Cup team's rubber training suit

"For the people back home, they are mad about rugby ... everyone is glued to TVs in the cities. In the villages maybe they have got together and got one TV and a generator and a ssatellite dish to pick up TV."

JOHN McKEE, Fiji coach, before they played England in the 2015 Rugby World Cup

"Whatever happens to us will be positive. It's like having a baby – before you have it, you don't know what it will look like. We are hoping the baby will be beautiful."

Georgia manager **ZAZA KASSACHVILI** asked whether he thought his team were in for a hammering in their opener against England, which they were

"At Murrayfield in 1990 we were a bunch of headless chickens. This time we kept cool. There is steel in this team and it is more experienced."

RORY UNDERWOOD after England beat Scotland 9-6 at Murrayfield in the 1991 World Cup semi-final.

CHAPTER 6

ROARING WITH THE LIONS

"A major rugby tour by the British Isles to New Zealand is a cross between a medieval crusade and a prep school outing."

JOHN HOPKINS British journalist

"I have been through some experiences in my rugby life but it is fair to say what happened to me in the Lions' scrum during our first Test was among the worst."

PHIL VICKERY, in 2009, after being destroyed by Springbok prop Tendai "The Beast" Mtawarira

"'The Beast' was pretty impressive. There was one scrum after nine minutes when we got lifted off the floor and if I was their scrum coach I would have retired and gone to Panama."

GRAHAM ROWNTREE, Lions scrumming coach on the 2009 Tour

"There's no point in drawing inspiration from the past. We have to live in the here and now."

SHAUN EDWARDS, Lions defence coach

"To play the game, you have to play on the edge, but unfortunately he's gone to the edge of the cliff and jumped off it."

Lions coach **WARREN GATLAND** on England's Dylan Hartley, whose 11-week ban for abusing a referee meant he missed the 2013 tour

"He is super-competitive and, at the end of the day, those are the guys you want beside you."

JONNY WILKINSON, after Lions fly-half Owen Farrell's temperament was questioned following an altercation with Saracens team-mate Schalk Brits

"I just kept going effortlessly, defenders seemed to fall off me, in fact I think I beat one bloke about 40 yards out and he came back to make another attempted tackle as I went over the line,"

JOHN BENTLEY in 1997 on his wonderful try against South Africa at Ellis Park

"That game yesterday was sick. And what McRae did was plain cowardly. I asked Ronan and he said he'd cleared McRae out at the ruck. Fairly, too. No punch, no kick. And then Ronan is punched. He thought he would just get the one, but then he takes another 10 cheap shots. That's way out of order."

AUSTIN HEALEY on Waratahs fullback Duncan McRae's unprovoked attack on Ronan O'Gara in 2015

"Willie John said before a game, against Transvaal, 'I need him to be demoralized.' He was talking about prop [Johan] Strauss, a real good 'un. We won 23-15 and taking off our boots, Willie John said, 'I see that man was done. His heart will never be mended. With the Springboks, that stays with them for ever.' He was right."

MIKE BURTON on the match against Transvaal in 1974

"In Cape Town for the first Test, in the captain's room nobody's saying a word. Willie John arrives, nobody says a word. And then 20 minutes passed! You can imagine the atmosphere in the room, and he just looked at us all and said: 'Right then, we're ready'. We got on the coach. The tension that had built up was fantastic."

England and Lions prop **FRAN COTTON** before the first Test in South Africa in 1974

"Syd [Millar] would ask you, 'What are you doing this afternoon?' You'd say, 'We're all going to have a drink.' You'd be in one of the boys' bedrooms and he'd come around about five o'clock and say, 'Hi, are you all right, men? Tomorrow's training schedule starts at eight – and we have a tough one.' That was his way."

MIKE BURTON, 1974

"I know it sounds strange, but in a way it was about love."

England No.8 **ANDY RIPLEY** may not have played in 1974 but he shouted himself hoarse from the touchline

"I'd never seen such chaos. We had 12 of us in rucks at times. We were literally all over the place."

JONNY WILKINSON reflects on the disastrous 2005 tour

"New Zealand sports fans are among the most arrogant in the world."

Former Lions lock **BEN KAY** on touring New Zealand in 2005

"I was just trying to keep my bind up, obviously. We talk about always, as a front row, giving good pictures to the referee and either I bind there or I drop my arm [and] it's a penalty to them. So I'd rather grab them than grab nothing, really."

Lions prop **MAKO VUNIPOLA** fools no-one explaining why he ended up grappling with Owen Franks' tender bits at Eden Park

"It's about character this week for us. It's about manning up and putting everything on the line, because it's that situation isn't it, it's do or die for us."

Lions assistant **ANDY FARRELL** sums up the stakes before the final test in New Zealand in 2017

"Like a Porsche passing a Lada."

RORY UNDERWOOD describes how his brother
Tony passed All Black legend John Kirwan in the 1993
Second Test in Wellington

"It's great to be part of the England scrum."

Ireland prop **NIGEL POPPLEWELL** when he was the only non-English forward in the British & Irish Lions team which won the second Test at Wellington in 1993

"What a kick in the teeth for a guy who has just lost his dad."

New Zealand RFU official **JOHN DOWLING**, after
Wade Dooley is denied permission to rejoin the 1993
Lions after he had to go home to bury his father

"It looks as if Iron Mike has gone a bit rusty."

Scotland flanker **JOHN JEFFREY**, about England's "Iron" Mike Teague on the 1989 British & Irish Lions tour to Australia

CHAPTER 7

CELEBRITY FANS

"I prefer rugby to soccer. I enjoy the violence in rugby, except when they start biting each other's ears off."

ELIZABETH TAYLOR in 1972

"My dresser and I have the hots for the new rugby ace Danny Cipriani. We have a shrine in my dressing room – press photos of him on the field looking swarthy and fit, and snaps of our boy emerging from Mayfair nightclubs, looking sexy and dishevelled."

Actor **JULIAN CLARY** on English rugby's new bad-boy pin-up

"Rugby is a good occasion for keeping thirty bullies far from the centre of the city."

OSCAR WILDE

"Rugby is a hooligans game played by gentlemen."

WINSTON CHURCHILL

"Rugby is a game for big buggers. If you're not a big bugger, you get hurt. I wasn't a big bugger, but I was a fast bugger and therefore I avoided the big buggers."

SPIKE MILLIGAN

"Playing rugby at school I once fell on a loose ball and, through ignorance and fear, held on despite a fierce pummelling. After that it took me months to convince my team-mates I was a coward."

Comedian **PETER COOK** in 1970

"Rugby is a game for the mentally deficient. That is why it was invented by the British. Who else but an Englishman could invent an oval ball?"

PETER COOK

"Rugby is what me and my son do together. We go to watch Wasps home or away, and we watch England, home or away. That's what we do together. The best thing I ever did for him was take him to rugby at five years old. It's the best thing I ever did for us as father and son."

GREG WALLACE, *Masterchef* judge

"Rugby is the most vicious sport on god's earth."

Boxer **CHRIS EUBANK**

"I played for years. I played scrum-half for about five or six years until I got too tall and instead of being a forward I elected to be a fly-half. I had to give up after numerous injuries but I'm like a Labrador with a tennis ball as soon as I see a rugby ball."

Enthusiastic England supporter **PRINCE HARRY**

"Tough but epic game @ChrisRobshaw. Still all to play for against Oz. Hope Wales can get backline together for Fiji!"

Hollywood actor **SAMUEL L JACKSON** tweets a hitherto unsuspected devotion to English rugby during the 2015 World Cup

"I have enjoyed going to Twickenham more than I have enjoyed watching football."

DAVID BECKHAM

"Gonna watch the rugby with my dad tonight and bro down."

ED SHEERAN during the 2015 Rugby World Cup

"Whoso would be a man, must be a non-conformist, and preferably play in the pack."

RALPH WALDO EMERSON shows his preference for piano moving over piano playing

"The pub is as much a part of rugby as is the playing field."

JOHN DICKINSON

"My England man put rampant rabbits to shame."

Tabloid headline for a piece based on a conversation with **ANGEL BARBIE**, one of the Kiwi girls entertained by England's finest in Auckland in 2008.

"Ok minutes to go before #ITAvENG be interesting to see how much Italy has improved since last 6 Nations. I am not a singer but I can hum 'Swing Low Sweet Chariot' all together now. Prediction from me an England win after early heavy pressure from Italy what do you think?"

Boxer **FRANK BRUNO MBE**, tweets before England met Italy in the Six Nations at Twickenham, February 2018

"I love rugby. Maybe now it is my second sport – I like in rugby the fact that kind of true solidarity. If you want to play, you have first to be together if you want to play. That is a quality I love in team sport and maybe nowhere better than in rugby.

Former Arsenal FC manager **ARSENE WENGER**

"The discipline is crucial, the teamwork, the respect for others. It doesn't matter where you are, it's all the same values. It brings the most amazing people together and opens your eyes to things you wouldn't really think about otherwise."

PRINCE HARRY, patron of the RFU,, on rugby's values

"They did it @englishrugby made the competitive decision. Holy s**t the @2015_RWC is on."

RUSSELL CROWE's excited tweet on Sam Burgess's controversial selection in England's 2015 World Cup squad. He co-owns Burgess's Australian RL team.

CHAPTER 8

TWICKENHAM HQ

"Twickenham's just a ground until it's filled up with fans."

DEWI MORRIS, former England scrum-half

"If the game is run properly as a professional game, you do not need 57 old farts running rugby."

WILL CARLING endears himself to the blazerati in 1995

"Bill, there's a bird just run on with your bum on her chest!"

England scrum-half **STEVE SMITH** to his skipper Bill Beaumont when streaker Erica Roe ran onto the pitch at Twickenham in 1982

"A bomb under the West car park at Twickenham on an international day would end fascism in England for a generation."

GEORGE ORWELL

"Rugby is not like tea, which is good only in England, with English water and English milk. On the contrary, rugby would be better, frankly, if it were made in a Twickenham pot and warmed up in a Pyrenean cauldron."

Frenchman **DENNIS LALANNE** in 1960

"The relationship between the Welsh and the English is based on trust and understanding. They don't trust us and we don't understand them."

DUDLEY WOOD, RFU secretary, the year before the first World Cup in 1987

"Houses, horses, cars, women. I'll trade anything for tickets. If you're a woman, I'll get you a man."

Former England prop turned ticket-fixer **MIKE BURTON**, the scourge of the RFU

"I didn't see the punch until it was shown on TV."

England lock **PAUL ACKFORD** after being laid out by at Twickenham by teenage Argentine prop Federico Mendez in 1990

"We are determined to retain the fundamental principles of amateurism within the English game. The RFU believes rugby should be played as a spare time activity for enjoyment and not for reward. The International Board's decision has completely undermined the essential amateurism of the game."

The RFU's **MIKE PEAREY** on the IRB's 1990 decision to allow players to earn money from peripheral marketing activities

"Someone calculated that we would need 74 days away this year for England matches alone. The balancing act between work and family is becoming impossible."

England lock **PAUL ACKFORD**, in 1991, as demands on players made professionalism ever more likely

"There's something in the spirit of rugger that's worth defining, difficult though it is to express."

LORD WAVELL WAKEFIELD, 1920s England captain and post-war RFU Secretary, was an enthusiastic custodian of the sport's amateur ethos

"There's a supposed amateur ethos, which I don't think really exists. That won't last for long. Come the next World Cup this game will be semi-professional. A lot of people won't like that, a lot of people will."

BRIAN MOORE, England hooker, thinks Rugby Union was on the cusp of professionalism, 1993

"Rugby must always be amateur, which means playing in one's spare time for recreation. If a man wants to play professional rugby, good luck to him. But there's no room for him in our game."

LORD WAKEFIELD, who died 10 years earlier, begged to differ

"Ritchie shouldn't be anywhere near it. I'm staggered."

SIR CLIVE WOODWARD learning RFU chief executive Ian Ritchie, who had extended Stuart Lancaster's contract, would sit on the 2015 World Cup review panel

"I only jump on the other side of the field. Then the selectors can see my number as I go up."

Quins lock **JOHN CURRIE** explains why he only jumped at lineouts on the far touchline during an England trial at Twickenham

"To be branded a professional after I had been regarded as a pillar of the establishment was quite ironic. I felt very bitter about it."

BILL BEAUMONT, on being banished for writing his autobiography

"Rugby's values of Teamwork, Respect, Enjoyment, Discipline and Sportsmanship are what makes the game special for those who enjoy the environment and culture they create. They define the game and define England Rugby."

The **RUGBY FOOTBALL UNION's** core values

"Women sit, getting colder and colder, on a seat getting harder and harder, watching oafs, getting muddier and muddier."

VIRGINIA GRAHAM, US social commentator and author, referring to the "muddied oafs" image conjured up by Rudyard Kipling's 1903 poem "The Islanders"

"The advantage law is the best law in rugby, because it lets you ignore all the others for the good of the game."

Author **DEREK ROBINSON**

"I couldn't very well hit him could I? I had the ball in my hands."

TOMMY BISHOP in trouble when he was charged
with kicking an opponent

"We cannot get too ahead of ourselves. We are only the number two team in the world and we want to be number one."

England coach **EDDIE JONES**